This Book Belongs to

....

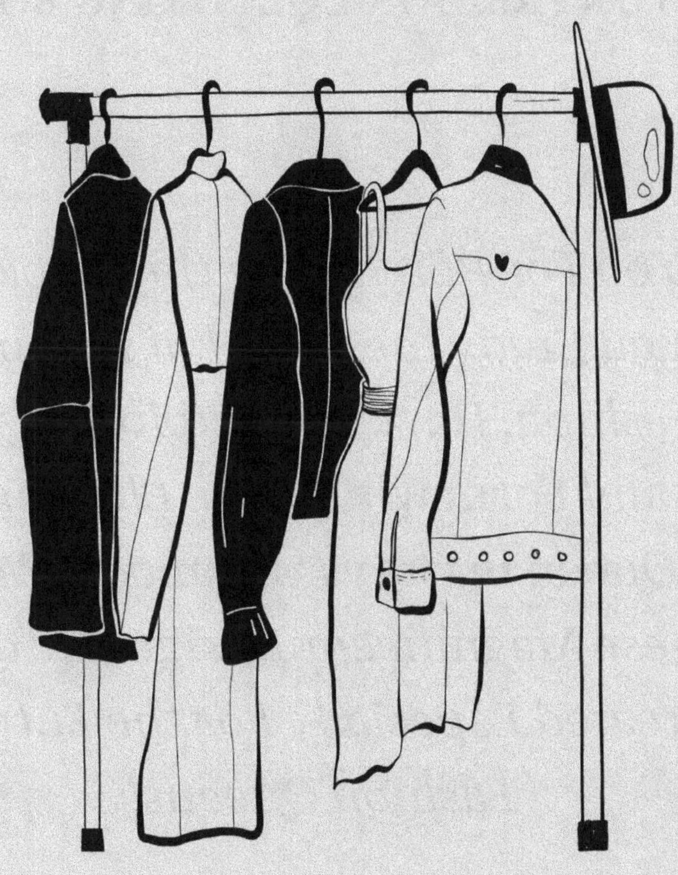

Fashion Queen

BE A QUEEN OF FASHION

A FUN FASHION COLOURING BOOK

Thank You For Purchasing this Book and We
Hope You Enjoy the World of Inspiration in
Design, Fashion. Have Fun Exploring your Style,
Colour and Form with these Elegant Fashion
Queen in Grayscale and B&W.
Bring These Magnificent Designs into Full Life.
Created Especially For the Future
Fashion Queens!

Draw & Design Your Own

DRAW & DESIGN YOUR OWN

DRAW & DESIGN YOUR OWN

DRAW & DESIGN YOUR OWN

DRAW & DESIGN YOUR OWN

DRAW & DESIGN YOUR OWN

DRAW & DESIGN YOUR OWN

DRAW & DESIGN YOUR OWN

DRAW & DESIGN YOUR OWN

DRAW & DESIGN YOUR OWN

DRAW & DESIGN YOUR OWN

DRAW & DESIGN YOUR OWN

DRAW & DESIGN YOUR OWN

DRAW & DESIGN YOUR OWN

DRAW & DESIGN YOUR OWN

DRAW & DESIGN YOUR OWN

DRAW & DESIGN YOUR OWN

DRAW & DESIGN YOUR OWN

DRAW & DESIGN YOUR OWN

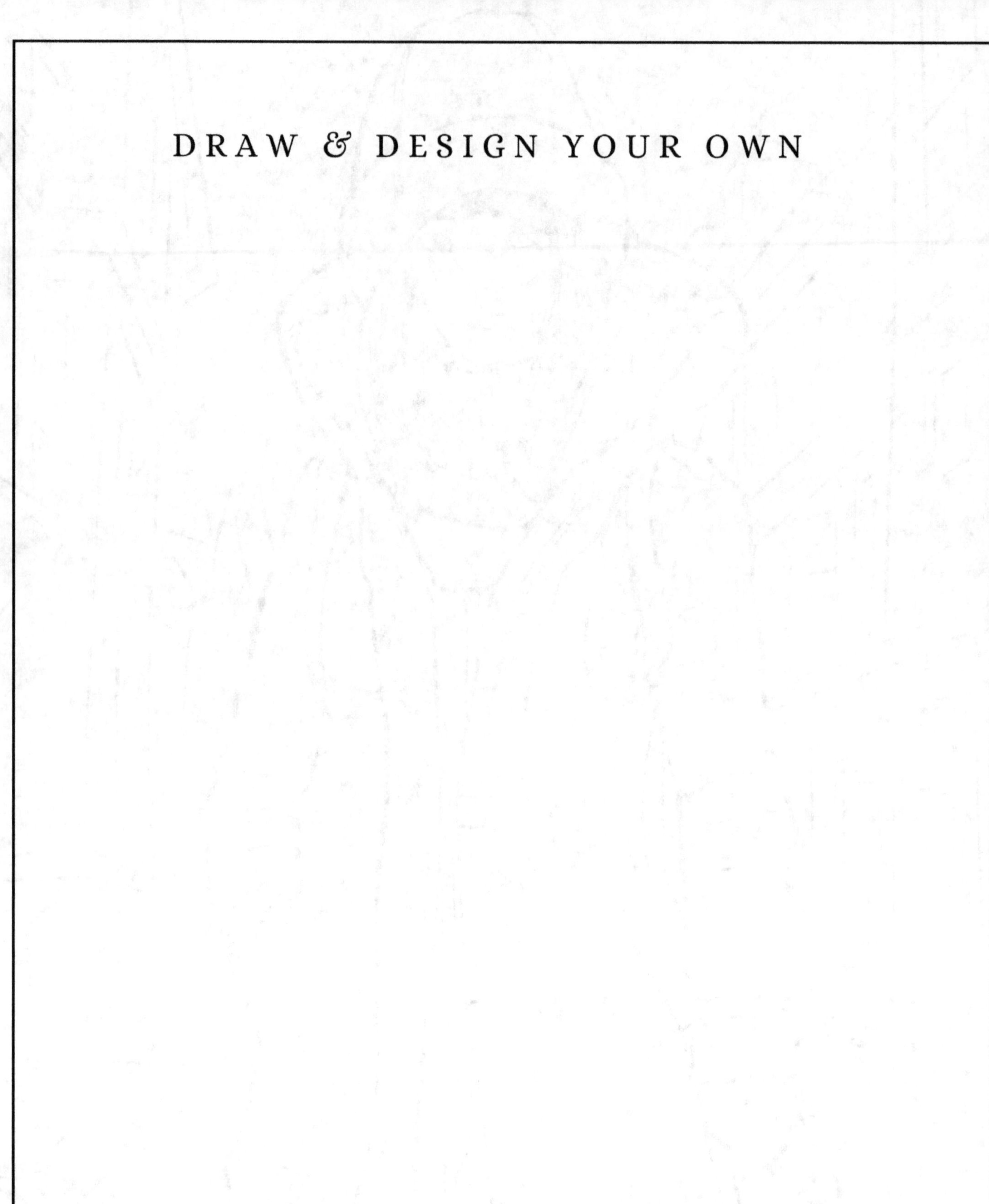

DRAW & DESIGN YOUR OWN

DRAW & DESIGN YOUR OWN

DRAW & DESIGN YOUR OWN

DRAW & DESIGN YOUR OWN

DRAW & DESIGN YOUR OWN

DRAW & DESIGN YOUR OWN

DRAW & DESIGN YOUR OWN

www.ingramcontent.com/pod-product-compliance
Lightning Source LLC
Chambersburg PA
CBHW081522250726
48659CB00009B/2906